Kelly Holmes
My Olympic Ten Days

Virgin BOOKS

First published in Great Britain in 2004 by
Virgin Books Ltd, Thames Wharf Studios
Rainville Road, London W6 9HA

A catalogue record for this book is available from the British Library.

ISBN 1 85227 222 8

Designed by Smith & Gilmour
Printed and bound in the UK by Bath Press, CPI Group

Contents

Foreword

The Olympics to any sporting person is the pinnacle of your career, the ultimate sporting event in the world. For me, it is even more than that: it is years of dreaming, dedication and determination. To be an Olympic champion is a dream that can take over your life, as mine did. When I used to think about it coming true I would always smile, but the thought that my Olympic dream would never come true was something unbearable. I have so much passion for what I do and I have never given up. After years of injury problems and struggling to keep my focus, having another tear of a calf muscle or having an operation that would put me out for a few weeks, I hoped that one year I would finally be given one bit of good luck instead of what I thought was a curse.

The Olympic Games have been filled with mixed emotions for me. I have been to three. The first was in 1996 in Atlanta, USA, which ended up a disaster, though there was a positive but painful angle to go with it. Going into the Games with a stress fracture was hardly the route I had planned for my first Olympics but finishing fourth in the 800 metres provided me with a huge amount of confidence that I would take on board for the years to come.

Four years later it was the Olympic Games in Sydney, Australia, and this time I had another major dilemma. I had a bad start to the season and I had only six weeks of major preparation. I won a bronze medal in the 800 metres. At the time it was gold; but gold is not gold until you have it.

I hoped that one day I would be given the chance to prove to myself that I have what it takes to be the athlete that I wanted to be – the best in the world. Throughout the years as a senior athlete I had won medals at the Olympics, World Championships, Commonwealth Games and European Championships, but I had also had seven years of injury problems. Could I keep going?

Athens was my time to shine: the birthplace of the Olympics and all the history that goes alongside the Games being staged in Greece. I dedicated myself to getting to these Games injury-free, that was my priority and my only chance of getting close to achieving my dream.

The Olympics are different from any other championship because there is an element of the unknown. I go to major championships every year and to make it to them is a feat in itself, but when you talk about the Olympics, it's special. Winning at the Olympics is the ultimate achievement in sport, something that goes down in the history books forever. It's not about the glory or the fame, it is about personal pride and perseverance.

I have always said that dreams can come true, you just never know when. If I had given up on mine, I would never have known whether this was true.

Since I have been back in Britain, I have been overwhelmed by the public's response, support and enthusiasm. I thank you all. It has been amazing and wonderful. I hope this diary will be a great reminder for everyone who was living my dream with me.

I would like to dedicate the book to two people who are part of my Olympic story: Alison Rose (Ali) my physiotherapist and Zara Hyde Peters of UK Athletics. Alison gave me so much support, commitment and friendship; she was my confidante and showed me dedication and loyalty, without which I may never have made it to these Olympic Games. Zara was my supporter, mother and friend. She kept me focused. She was the rock I needed to get me to the end of my quest. Without her, I may never have become a legend.

You will both always be part of making my dream come true.

OLYMPIC 800 METRES AND 1,500 METRES CHAMPION, NOVEMBER 2004

History of Women in the Olympics

Since the age of twelve, when my P.E. teacher, Debbie Page at Hugh Christie School in Kent, made the suggestion that I might have a talent for running, this sport has played a part in my life. But winning two gold medals this year in the Olympic Games was an achievement that even I could not have anticipated. I had always strived towards being the best, reaching the ultimate goal, but now, when people say Kelly Holmes, Britain's greatest woman Olympian, it is hard to take in.

What is also hard to imagine is a life without running. Or at least the competitive side that drives me on and brings out emotions in me that I never knew existed.

I have been competing on the international stage for more than a decade and only when I think back and digest how far women's running and women's middle distance running in the Olympics has progressed, do I realise that I was lucky to be born in this era.

Thirty years ago I would not have been able to run the 1,500 metres at the Olympic Games; fifty years ago I would not have been able to do the 800 metres. Such has been the development of equal rights for women on the Olympic stage that, in Athens this year, there were more than one hundred events in which women competed. Dare anyone suggest we do not have the stamina?

But that is exactly what people did say at the end of the nineteenth century and the start of the twentieth, when the modern era of the Olympics was born. How ironic it is.

In Athens, at this year's Olympics, some of the women's events produced the best drama, but in 1896, at the first modern Olympics, women were not even allowed to compete in the Games.

And it used to be even worse. The history books tell us that in the ancient Games, women were even banned from attending as spectators – and if they did, the result would be death! Those that tried to break the rules, by dressing up as men, were thrown over a cliff for defying the authorities.

Baron Pierre de Coubertin, the man who created the modern Olympics, was against women competing. They did not in 1896, but were part of the occasion four years later in Paris in specific events such as yachting and tennis. Incredibly, though, it was not until 1928 that athletics for women became part of the programme.

Not that there were many events. There were the 100 metres, the 4x100 metres relay, the high jump and the discus ... and the 800 metres. And rarely could there have been a more controversial two-lap race in the history of the Olympics. The 1928 Games were held in Amsterdam, the Dutch city where today, ironically, international athletics is hardly ever staged. Middle distances were not run very often by women, but the final of the 800 metres was a tremendous race and a world record was set by Germany's Lina Radke, who won in 2:16.8. The world record today is 1:53.28.

The finish of the eighth heat of the Women's Olympic 100 metre dash in 1928. Myrtle Cook of Canada (left) won the race, second place was taken by Miss Wilson of New Zealand (right) and third by Miss Horst of Holland (centre).

However, the race has stayed part of the folklore of women's distance running and, while it is not exactly the topic that gets talked about between women athletes prior to a race, we should sometimes realise how times have changed.

Nowadays we have the opportunity to express ourselves on the track and make careers out of being professional runners over distances that were unheard of for women runners in the past.

Yes, Amsterdam in 1928 was some occasion. When the final finished, some women collapsed with exhaustion, some had to be helped away from the track and the anti-feminist brigades had a field day. The International Amateur Athletic Federation was of the theory that women should not run further than 200 metres and the *Daily Mail* newspaper even said that any strenuous running could age a woman.

A survey not so long ago claimed that by the middle of the next century, women might be sprinting faster than men, yet if the International Olympic Committee had had their way in 1928, the role of women in the sport would not have progressed.

Comte de Baillet Latour, the president of the IOC, actually wanted to remove all women's sports from the Olympics, but people pointed out that men also actually faint occasionally in sporting events. But the IAAF had their say and any women's races longer than 200 metres were banned from the Olympics – and they did not return until 1960.

Not that women did not run longer distances in those intervening 32 years. They did and slowly the sport developed. In 1960, in Rome, the women's 800 metres returned to the Olympic fold. The Russian Lyudmyla Shevtsova won the 800 metres in 2:04.3 that year and then four years later Ann Packer of Great Britain won in Tokyo.

Throughout the last forty years, the power and strength of women running the middle distance in the Olympic Games has grown and has anyone aged dramatically because of the exhaustion? Victory is usually met with a gold medal, not grey hairs. I train with men and how can we forget that, when Paula Radcliffe broke the marathon world record in London last year, her time was quicker than many members of the opposite sex.

Maria Mutola, my training partner, took the 800 metres to a new level in the modern era with her amazing record in places such as Zurich, where she has won for twelve successive years, and her dominance prior to Athens of the major championships.

In 1972 in Munich, women were allowed to run the 1,500 metres at the Olympics for the first time. It had been run at the European Championships three years earlier as gradually more women moved into the longer events. Nowadays, as in Athens, there are six heats in the first round of the 800 metres. What does that tell us? There is no question that the standard of women's middle distance running is improving as the athlete of today becomes stronger and the opposition becomes greater. It meant the double became achievable. Later in the book we will look at Tatyana Kazankina and Svetlana Masterkova, the Russian women who won both the 800 metres and 1,500 metres at the Olympics of 1976 and 1996 respectively. On the back of the 800 metres and 1,500 metres becoming established events at the Olympic Games, the women's marathon was staged for the first time in Los Angeles in 1984, the 10,000 metres was held in Seoul in 1988 and, in 1996 in Atlanta, the 5,000 metres was introduced, succeeding the 3,000 metres.

In England I train with Andy Graffin and, before these Olympics, when we were at the team's camp in Cyprus, I was working with Tony Whiteman. They are both British internationals and, in this era, training with men can help to take you that bit further. My training is well within their capability and, however I run, they can adapt and there will always be consistency. I trained a lot more with guys this year; it suits me and it worked because they are stronger and I was able to push myself much harder.

Never mind women not being allowed to run at the Olympics. This one has two gold medals to show for it from ten days that changed my life.

Ludmila Bragina setting a new world record and winning the gold medal for the women's 1,500 metres at the 1972 Olympic Games in Munich.

My Olympic Diary

Day One
Thursday, 19 August

THE SOUND OF MUSIC

Now I know it is real. Welcome to the Olympic Games. We are in the village. What a huge place. Vast. People dashing about everywhere, all off in different directions but all in search of that same goal: to have a great Olympic games. It does not matter whether they are shooters or canoeists or cyclists or gymnasts. We are like one big family who all wants to reach that same target.

I am settling in well. We are in an apartment in the British block. There are five of us sharing: Kelly Sotherton, who is competing in the heptathlon, Tracey Morris and Liz Yelling, who are running the marathon, Jo Pavey who is doing the 5,000 metres and 1,500 metres and myself. Goldie Sayers (javelin) and Kathy Butler (10,000 metres) are expected to arrive later in the week. We have all been in Cyprus at the British team's holding camp. The weather was superb, acclimatising us for the conditions here in Athens and I am feeling fantastic. My last few training sessions could not have gone better. I don't want to tempt fate with my track record but I have never felt better prior to the start of a major championship.

I am injury free. It is wonderful.

The Olympics opened six days ago. We were still in Cyprus at the time and the athletics programme starts tomorrow. I am racing in the evening. I have been trying to concentrate on my own preparation and I have watched little of the other Olympic sports on television.

Three days ago I decided I was going to run the 800 metres. I had been debating about it. The 1,500 metres, which starts next week, had been my first choice but I am going to double up because I feel good and I have been running well. It is going to be some task, mainly because the heats of the 1,500 metres begin the day after the final of the 800 metres, which I hope I will be in. Who knows whether I have made the right choice? But I feel relaxed and there is a fabulous atmosphere in our Olympic home.

Denise Lewis is staying in the apartment below ours; Paula Radcliffe is next door. Everyone is a bit apprehensive and looking forward to starting.

We keep putting these notes on each other's doors to wish everyone good luck. It is a big day for Kelly Sotherton tomorrow. It is her first Olympics. I must write her another message. The camaraderie between us all is fantastic. We all feel at home. I made sure the room was to my liking the moment I arrived. Kelly, Jo and I have a room each – Jo is next door to me, but Liz and Tracey are sharing.

I wanted to make the room feel like 'mine', so I changed all the furniture around. I put the two beds together to make them look like a double and the same with the two wardrobes. All that noise, God knows what it sounded like downstairs!

I am lying on the bed. I look around my room. I feel comfortable. I have had loads of cards and letters and have put them on the door and wardrobes. Some of the words in the greetings from people are so kind, so warm, wishing me luck. The support from outside has been fantastic.

But I cannot allow anything to break my concentration. I have to forget what else is happening. In 24 hours' time everything I have worked for this season will be geared into my first race, the 800 metres. What a feeling. I want it to be like that when I step out onto the Olympic track tomorrow night with nothing to concern me except my race.

Since we arrived here, the atmosphere has been great, but I can feel a different vibe around the place today. As the competition starts tomorrow, some people, such as Kelly, will be competing in the morning. I am trying to stay composed. My race is not until night-time. If I panic, I am wasting energy and I am not staying focused on what I am doing. I relax by playing music and I have decided that there is one song that I am going to use throughout the Olympics: 'If I Ain't Got You' by Alicia Keys.

The words are wonderful, so inspirational…

Some people want diamond rings
Some just want everything
But everything means nothing
If I ain't got you.

Brilliant! Whatever happens in the days ahead, those words are going to be all about the medals I am going to attempt to win. I am going to play the song non-stop and everyone else will be fed up with it.

I have decided that the dog tags that we were given by Ben Sherman when we received our official British Olympic clothes will be my lucky charm.

Here I am. No turning back now, Kelly. It is official, in print on the start list which has been handed to me. I am racing at 22.12 tomorrow night. My Olympic Games begin then.

The main thing is to ensure I qualify from the first round without hassle. I have decided that I will not look too much in depth about who I am racing against.

The first three qualify from each heat plus a number of the fastest losers and I am in the same race as Jearl Miles Clark of the USA and Tamsyn Lewis, the Australian champion.

I rested yesterday but today I am going to do some drills and acceleration.

Margo Jennings, my coach, and Jeff Fund, my agent, are with Maria Mutola. Maria runs for Mozambique and Margo had said that she would not be able to be in both camps if I decided to do the 800 metres. She has coached Maria for fourteen years. The Mozambique Federation have brought Margo out here, so I don't have her around.

Zara Hyde Peters, UK Athletics' development officer, and Alan Storey, who coaches Sonia O'Sullivan among others, are really cool and, as I get ready for the 1,500 metres, things will change when Margo comes back into the fold.

Bruce Hamilton, one of the team doctors, and I are going through the procedures for each of my races. I am concerned that I am not going to have enough time to recover, because the 800 metres final is the day before the first heats of the 1,500 metres. We decide that the best thing is to have a recovery pack at the track after each race. I will make up a carbo drink, protein drink, rehydration drink and a ham and cheese roll. I will get them ready tonight and be prepared for tomorrow.

I have great support behind me and I am making sure I see the people each day who will help me keep my head together: Zara, my physiotherapist Alison (Ali) Rose, Bruce, the other team doctor Bryan English and Alan Storey, who is here when I need him.

Ali will be at the track. I have been working with her for a long time and think that as soon as I come off she can do my ice rubs and massages.

The schedule I have is going to be pretty demanding on my body. Will I make it? I am going to make it, I tell myself.

It is time to go to the track. I miss the team meeting. Zara will fill me in.

Unlike Sydney's village there are a couple of tracks in Athens which is great, but I don't want to do that much walking around because I have a long week ahead. I am going to go to one of the outside training tracks, which is a short bus ride away.

There are loads of people at the track and now there really is this feeling of 'here we go'. The session involves fifteen minutes of warm-ups with some stretching and accelerating strides and my various drills. It is a routine I go through before I race and train.

I stick to the same programme as usual. I put my spikes on for some sprints. I feel good and I have had people telling me that I look in great shape. I have lost five kilograms this year, which is strange for me. I am ready to go.

I am looking forward to the first round. I don't know how it will all pan out in the Games, but I am confident in my ability to make the final and feel I am capable of getting a medal. In a few days we shall find out the answers, but here on this evening in Athens, what an exciting journey we are all about to undertake. What an adventure!

During training, something really odd happens. Margo, Jeff and Maria are all there. But I have to act like they are not and focus on myself. It makes me feel stronger and better, not having to rely on anyone and being able to focus on what I have to achieve. It is weird not having that interaction with your coach and Maria, the person who has been my training partner all last year. But I feel it might be a benefit for me. We shall see.

Tonight I'm going to have an ice bath after I have seen Ali. Normally it is good for my recovery. It worked in Cyprus and it is probably best for me to carry on with that. Ali has been fantastic. I have put my faith in her and without her I would not be in my best shape. She was in Cyprus the whole time I was there and it gave me the confidence to push my body that bit harder, enabling me to feel I had the right support.

I have had some niggles with my ankles and lower back, and a neural sensation in my leg. The best thing is to keep on top of everything. I have a hard nine days ahead. I want to go into this race feeling loose and ready. I have had a minor problem with my breathing and Ali has been working on my upper back. She has given me some serious treatment there. It hurts but it helps.

Now for the ice bath. These are in the cellar of one of the blocks. I am in this dingy place and I am on my own. There are three or four normal dustbins, a huge ice machine and only one light. It is not the best place to be. In fact, it is a bit scary. Shall I stay or shall I go? The ice buckets are here and I suppose I have to do it.

I always scream my head off when I first get into the ice before I get used to it. I think I am allergic to cold. But what do I expect. It is an ice bath!

I have been so focused during all the build-up and at the holding camp that I feel like my body is totally at its peak. Now is the time for me to perform.

I go to the dinner hall, which is huge. But, and here is the only downside of the village, the food is not as good as it was in Sydney at the last Olympics. We had so many choices there. You can always find something you like, though. Here there is salmon, pasta and salad but what I really want is an early night.

I am going to take a sleeping tablet. I don't normally do that before I race, but the doctor recommended it because I haven't been sleeping very well and need my rest. I do not compete until late the next night, so it is more important that I have a good night's sleep.

I have been playing my song. Tomorrow night the Olympics start for me. Every night before I race I have a ritual. I set out on the bed all that I need, no matter what. I have my moss spikes, crop top, my shorts, my numbers, my tracksuit and my extra numbers for bags and tracksuit. I am happy, I am settled. Hopefully now I am going to get a good night's sleep because a big day awaits.

I have been so focused during all the build-up and at the holding camp that I feel like my body is totally at its peak.

19

Day Two
Friday, 20 August

INTO THE UNKNOWN

Brilliant! I slept much better last night. It must have been the mild sleeping tablet. I don't feel drowsy but it does leave you with a metal mouth. As I am not racing until late tonight, I want to relax as much as possible. I will have a stretch and a massage. It is great that for once my body needs minimal work. But I will leave the ice bath until after the race.

I am going to have a late lunch because I have a long day ahead. I don't tend to eat loads and loads before I race, but not eating enough is not good because, by the time I get to race, I might have used up all my energy, possibly through nerves, and that will have a bad effect.

That song. I have listened to it three times already this morning and it is inspiring me more than anything else.

Barring anything major going wrong – me falling over or something – I hope I will qualify for the second round. My main objective later is to suss out the warm-up procedure, making sure I give myself enough time for the bus ride, finding out what the warm-up area is like, where the call room is, where you have to go before the race. Generally feeling my feet. I watch a little bit of the Olympics today, the diving is great and I have seen Kelly in the heptathlon. She was up early and she has started well in her competition. She is looking good.

I am becoming a little bit nervy, probably because I want to get going. I am in the right frame of mind: I am in race mode.

I don't like to talk to many people. I have not spoken to Margo. That is fine. Zara and Ali have been a good support team and every bit of confidence I can get from them is great. I am always saying to people: do you think I can do this, are you sure I can do that, what if this or that happens?

Ali has been telling me that I am in the best shape of my life physically which is true. I have had no major problems all year. I have to qualify, whatever happens.

21

My mind-set puts me in the right mood for the big championships, rather than just odd races where the goal is winning. I like to have big challenges.

All the athletes have different people taking them down to the Olympic Stadium. My chaperone is Zara. The British are very good like that. I have seen a lot of countries' teams that are disorganised. I hope Zara will be my chaperone all week because I like to have a routine when I get prepared, especially at the championships.

My mind-set puts me in the right mode for the big championships, rather than just odd races where the goal is winning. I like to have big challenges.

I am on the bus with Zara. She is talkative but I don't say much when I am going to race. She knows me now. She can keep on chatting and I will listen and I will nod when I want to nod. I am more nervous, mainly through apprehension and not knowing what the outcome will be. That is probably the worst thing for an athlete, and if you start thinking about it, then you worry. The bus ride takes 20 minutes, which is fine. Time to relax.

We reach the warm-up area and the British team are set up at the top of the two tracks. Ali is already down there and everyone knows now that I am in my race mode. I must be relaxed. Pedro, our masseur, and I have this little joke about the ringtone on Alan Storey's phone. We keep singing the tune to each other, which is making me laugh; normally I would not even be acknowledging anyone.

Jo Pavey is here; she runs tonight too. I find my little space and see Jo Fenn, who is in the 800 metres too. I hope she does well. People think that when you are in the same team and in the same event that you should be big rivals … I am not like that. Your performance is what you do on the track and no one can distract you from that. But what is wrong with being polite and supportive of other people?

I am here early. I wanted to make sure the bus was not late and to find out where the toilets are. Bryan (English) is in charge of my recovery pack and he will meet me in the mixed zone area when I come off of the track. It is where all the journalists are waiting to speak to athletes but I am not sure how big it is and how long it will be until I see him. I can work that out tonight and if I need to adjust it for tomorrow, I will.

I warm up on the lower track first because the grass is better. I do a fifteen-minute jog and there is that Alicia Keys song again. I am singing it out loud which is a bit embarrassing.

Some people live for the power, yeah
Some people live just to play the game

I know the words off by heart now. I will do my drills at the top track where all the physios are. I feel good. My legs feel brilliant, really springy. I am fast, snappy and I know it is my time to start racing.

I have another ritual that I go through. Zara has to put my numbers on; no one else is allowed to do it. I like to keep everything exactly the same. I am called up, the race is drawing closer, about 40 minutes away. There is no turning back. I feel ready to perform and hopefully it will go well. I want to feel good in the race because I'll know where I'll stand for the next day.

The first call room is like a tent. There are aisles with areas sectioned off and you have to assemble according to what heat you are in. They check your clothing because you are not allowed any extra branding or advertising other than what has been declared by your national team. The officials look at your spikes to make sure they are the correct length, five or six millimetres, and they also take away your mobile telephones and cameras. Perhaps they don't want people's phones ringing when they are out on the track. You are told to collect them after your race. Sometimes it can be quite obstructive and agitating when they are trying to take stuff from your bag and you are trying to keep your concentration. I stay as calm as possible and let them get on with it. It is the Olympic Games and I am not going to allow something like that to have a detrimental effect on me.

We are escorted down to the second call room. It is a long walk, a tunnel into the unknown. We are underneath the stadium. It is quiet. Everyone is anxious. In the heats and the semi-finals, you know you have to qualify, and I find these races more nerve-wracking than the final. Many of us have been through it many times before but every place is different and you don't quite know what to expect.

I have acknowledged Agnes Samaria. She is a friend of mine. She runs for Namibia. I hope she does well. She is running in the heat before me. The tension grows. It is the Olympic Games. The pinnacle of our careers.

It is the last chance to go to the toilet. There are Portaloo cabins at the back. Luxury! I go to the first one and have decided that will be the toilet that I will use in every single race. Everything has to be exactly the same.

23

People are putting on spikes and checking numbers. We are reminded what lane we will be in for the race – I am in three. They have been decided on season's best times for each athlete and it does not matter who is in the race. I put my spikes on and I am looking forward to racing but it is quite daunting. When they call you up to go, that is it – a massive arena with all the atmosphere and you are going to be part of the occasion.

The first thing I do when I go out onto the track is to find the official British flag flying in the stadium, but my eyesight is not too good lately. I am focusing. I am looking – yes, I can see it.

I am happy; I always like to do that when I step out at the Olympics. The British fans are amazing. I wave to some of them but then I go back into that zone, pretending it is literally just the runners and the track. It is hard, especially when you see hundreds of cameramen at the point where we are about to start, all the press to my right, the big screens, and fans cheering at the other events.

'Stay focused, Kelly,' I tell myself.

We are called to our lanes.

Bang! My Olympics has begun with my first race of (hopefully) six in nine days and I decide that I am going to be at the back of the pack. I figure my best way of racing from my 1,500 metre strength is to run as evenly-timed laps as possible. It looks like I am starting quite slow but the rest of the field is actually going quite fast.

I could be a second or even two seconds down over the first 200 metres and it seems I am trailing off the back of the pack. I always think that by the time I get to 400 metres, I have done it more efficiently than many of the others. I have not wasted early energy and what I save at the start of a race I will have at the end. You never know what is going to work for you.

I am hoping to stick to my plan. But you have to judge yourself as you go through the race.

Heats are not always fast races, although there are people on the borderline who might take themselves out to try to qualify as best as possible. You have to be cautious. The rest of us that feel we have the capability of qualifying and do not want to waste ourselves. We want to have at least as much energy left for the semis, which are the next day.[2]

I hang back from the pace; I relax as much as I can. My objective is always to look where the first three are, count them, know that is where I need to be and keep to my aim.

Along the back straight on the second lap, 250 metres from home, I make a move, so I am confident I am going to make it. I feel I am one of the fastest, especially over 1,500 metres, but in the 800 metres I am up against people who have been training for this distance all the time, so it means using all my strength.

I find the race is quite comfortable. I take my time, I win it and even I am surprised how good I feel.

I run up to the mixed zone. I see Sally Gunnell and I poke my tongue out at her as I run past. I don't usually get interviewed by the BBC TV at such an early stage of the competition and my objective is to get my rehydration pack as soon as possible. A lot of people are calling me. I speak to one or two journalists briefly. They ask me how I feel. I tell them 'Good' and run off.

I get my bag from Bryan. I start my protein drink straight away and I run up to the area where our kits have been taken. I start munching on my ham and cheese roll, which might not be the best thing to have when you have just finished a race but my priority is to replace my energy. I have been told to wear compression socks to help any inflammation in my legs. I put them on, I warm down, then I am on a table where Ali is giving me a massage and Bruce comes over to start an ice massage.

It has all happened within 25 minutes. I hope this routine will be one of the keys to me continuing throughout the championship.

We arrive at the village and head down to dinner. I have eaten and it is 1.30 a.m. I decide to have an ice bath. It's a late hour for it, but it is such a beneficial way of relaxing the muscles.

I would like to have a shower but everyone else in my apartment is asleep so I can't. It is not right to make too much noise. Kelly will be up early again for her event.

I go to bed without one – disgusting! But that is an athlete for you.

Day Three
Saturday, 21 August

CRUNCH TIME

AUGUST 19
AUGUST 20
AUGUST 21
3
1
2
4
5
6
7
8
9
10
AUGUST 22
AUGUST 23
AUGUST 24
AUGUST 25
AUGUST 26
AUGUST 27
AUGUST 28

How glad I am that yesterday is out of the way! When you first start Championships, you don't know what the procedure is. It is the semi-final tonight and I am feeling nervous but relaxed about this one. The first two runners up will qualify by rights, and I am actually worried whether I can qualify. Jearl Miles Clark is in my race again, as is Russian Tatyana Andrianova, who I do not know very much about. Jearl runs from the front and always pushes the pace, so I will have to be aware of that.

Semis are a real race: you have to make the final, while subconsciously you want to save a bit of energy for when you progress. So why hold back? At least tomorrow is a rest day. If you are flat out for that semi-final then so be it. I have to do it. I am in shape. But will I get through?

I always make sure I have fresh clothes to run in, which you can do at a championship because of the sets you are given. Today I have laid them all out. I have been trying to get a few crunch bars, they are easier to eat after the race than a ham and cheese roll.

I text Sally Gunnell. I worked out she was the first person I saw when I came off the track and have asked her to bring me some peanuts and have a bottle of water. She said fine, no problem. I want my recovery to begin within the first five minutes of me leaving the track. I have never done this before because normally you do not get to eat for at least 30 minutes after racing.

I am racing an hour-and-a half earlier tonight but it will be the same procedure. If I manage to progress through the rest of the championship, each race takes place at around this same time, between 8 and 9 p.m., so my build-up will be exactly the same. My legs feel good, I do not think I took anything out of them yesterday. They don't feel tired.

I have seen Ali. It is fantastic how all the effort is reaping dividends. I have had day-to-day treatment all year and my body has held up. I am not sure if it would have done had I not gone through this process. It is always good to hear people giving you positive thoughts, telling you that you can do it. Ali is great at that.

27

I have been quite sociable. I am not normally like that. Most times I have been to a championship, I have made it there after a real fight with injury. Not this year.

I am ready to race again, but I still have a good few hours to go. I have been watching the heptathlon on the television and I am sure Kelly (Sotherton) is on target to win a medal. It would be amazing if she did, this being her first Olympics.

I have been quite sociable. I am not normally like that. Most times I have been to a championship, I have made it there after a real fight with injury. Not this year. I have lunch with Agnes. It has all been going well for her. She made it through and I have been speaking to her about getting my hair done. I must feel confident. All is ready. I know the procedure, the rest is down to me.

I arrive at the track. As soon as I start warming up, the song is there in my head and hopefully people think I am just mumbling...

Some people want diamond rings
Some just want everything...

I do my drills. They are there to sharpen the legs, warm the hips and other parts of the body you don't normally use for regular running. I am in the first heat. I look at my opponents because you can get vibes from them, seeing if they are tired. They are looking confident and relaxed; so am I.

I spoke to Zara and she told me how the other runners progressed through their qualifying rounds. I am not sure if she was biased, but she says that I looked the best one out of them all.

You get a good idea who is in form. Benhassi (of Morocco) has a good finish, Ceplak (of Slovenia) has control, Mutola has so much experience. Semis are tough. My heat is one of the toughest, with Jearl and Tatyana. I am in lane four and it feels like it is a final.

I am in that first toilet again, the last bit of confined space before the race.

I am out on the track. I do a few strides around the top bend and people shout my name. When the race starts, I am at the back. It worked for me yesterday and I am going to go for that again.

Jearl used to be a 400 metre runner. She likes to burn others off and I have to be aware that she can do that. I will still be at the back for the first 200 metres but I am a bit closer in contact with the end people so that I do not allow a big gap to develop.

I want to run my own race. Tatyana is in the pack. I stay towards the back and, at 400 metres, Jearl is through in a fast time of 56 seconds. I am there in 58 seconds. I have saved that couple of seconds to the end of the race.

I make my move on the back straight.

1:57.98

I make my move on the back straight. I am into third place. We go around the top bend and all is going well. I am in the right place with 100 metres left, in contention and I end up winning the semi-final in 1:57.98 from Tatyana and Jearl.

I head straight to Sally. What a girl! She has remembered my peanuts and water. I eat them straightaway and, as I am talking to her, I am probably spitting them out everywhere. I keep my interviews brief. I do not want to think about what I was doing because I just want to do it. I know a lot of people thought, 'Why is she hiding?' I did not want to say much. I knew in my own mind that the best way to focus was to get on with it myself.

I warm down, I still feel bouncy. I am back earlier, so it is no problem. I am going to have a shower this time. I see Ali for some treatment and then head downstairs for an ice bath. It is not pleasant.

I am not tired. I am still on an adrenaline rush. I am pleased with how I raced and I feel really good about my chances in the 800 metres. Tomorrow is a rest day so there is no need for a sleeping pill tonight. I can allow myself to come down naturally.

All the hard work and intense volume of training that I did in Cyprus in the camp before the Games is paying off. Running two minutes for the 800 metres is feeling easy. Everything has a positive light shining upon it. **'**

Day Four
Sunday, 22 August

AND THE TIMETABLE SAID REST

What time is it? Gee, 2 a.m. and I cannot sleep. I am buzzing. I am hyper after being on such a high last night. I hear the door to our apartment open. Kelly Sotherton has returned home, all alone, except with something rather special – a bronze medal from her first Olympics. What a performance she produced last night to finish third in the heptathlon. I remember when I did that in Sydney four years ago. Coming back to the apartment having won bronze in the 800 metres, I thought everyone was in bed. It was horrible. I wanted to see somebody, you can imagine the excitement. I wanted to talk about it. Allison Curbishley was sitting in the shower on her telephone so not to disturb anyone and we stayed up for ages talking.

I am here awake and there is no way Kelly is going to be alone. I am going to see her. She has a bronze medal, and no one is there to celebrate with her. We have a good chat but I do not want to look at her medal. It is a jinx. I am really pleased for her, but ask her not to show it to me. She doesn't, she quickly wraps it up and puts it away. My 800 metres final is tomorrow and I am superstitious of everything I do. It is great to be able to share someone else's experience, though.

It is morning, well late morning that is. Not that I have slept much. I will eat properly and be fuelled up for the race tomorrow. Ah, the race, the final of the 800 metres. I am going to do my best not to think about it. I want to try to clear it from my mind because then I can stay relaxed.

I am going to see Ali to have a massage. I have so much faith in her. I will have an ice bath afterwards because when she massages me deeply, it is like giving inflammation to the muscles. It is better that I calm them down a bit straight away.

The big priority is to have my hair done today for the final. But I must get my washing sorted. We were given two little sacks, one is white and the other is blue, for our coloureds. I hand them to the village laundry.

I meet up with Agnes, who unfortunately did not make the final. I have known her for about four years. The 800 metre runners are all close. I have been training in South Africa; she lives near Frankie Fredericks in Namibia. I have been out to see her there and for the last year she has also been trained by Margo.

It is lunchtime and here is Kelly again. She has been doing all her press interviews and is really excited. She has flowers and Jo Pavey and I have some photos taken with her which is great. It makes the whole experience enjoyable. There is a great atmosphere in our apartment. Liz Yelling, who I stayed with in Cyprus, is here with us and we have been laughing the whole time, another important factor as to how I will react throughout the champs.

But in our apartment there has also been loads of excitement and nervous anticipation because it is the women's marathon this evening which both Liz and Tracey are running in. It has actually been quite an eye-opener watching the way they have prepared for the race, as someone who runs much shorter distances. They had got their drink bottles ready which have to be put out at the different points along the course and you have to recognise which one is yours are go by to collect it. Now that cannot be easy! Tracey put a Welsh flag on hers, Liz had a Union Jack sticking out and they had all these 5k and 10k markings over the bottles.

Tracey is so new to the game. She has just mucked in and does not have the nerves that most of us probably have. She was in the position of feeling half excited, half being in the unknown.

I have missed the start of the race. I am just concentrating my mind today. But I head to the physio room and a few of us are there, laying on the beds watching the marathon. We are glued to what is happening. Paula has not broken away. Maybe she has another tactic?

Not this time. She stops and there is a communal sigh of 'Oh, no.' It is heartbreaking to see her cry. I know how much it meant to her and how much she has put her life into trying to achieve gold at the Olympics and seeing her breaking down and not being able to respond is tough. There was so much pressure on Paula; the outside pressures were immense. I was upset for her and it made me think that my decision not to do any press interviews in Cyprus has worked well.

My goal was to get my head down and I had made that decision to perform. When Liz and Tracey arrive back, they are pleased. They both ran well and there is still this buzz in our apartment. There are a lot of girls who get medals but you have to remember that there are so many athletes here, that they all put in the same commitment, and a lot of people do not give them much recognition. Sharing with Liz, as I did in Cyprus, showed that she hardly ever got any mention about being in the Olympics in the build-up, after Tracey had broken through to qualify with her run in the London Marathon. Everyone kind of forgot about Liz. But she too had made the Olympic team for the first time in her career. It was a big thing. We all gave them great support in the apartment. They achieved some great results in the marathon.

I am concerned that I might not recover in time from tomorrow's final because the first round of the 1,500 metres is the next day. I talk to the doctors about a rehydration infusion, filled with minerals and magnesium to make sure my body recovers totally. I will have that, no matter what, after the 800 metres. But of course I cannot avoid what is happening tomorrow. It is one of the strongest women's 800 metre finals ever.

It will be tough. Can I put it to the back of my mind?

I have done my best to do so, but now, in the evening, I am going through my race plan with Zara. She has had a look at all the semi-finals rounds. I memorised what I did in the heats, she told me who she thought looked comfortable and who were the dangers.

I have just received another text from my old coach Dave Arnold who has been a great influence throughout my career. He says: *Hi Kelly. You were most impressive in the semi finals. Cioncan: strong, but no speed. Clark: you have beaten. Ceplak: may take it out, but could change her game plan. Mutola: doesn't look as dominant, but she can barge and has a lot of experience – you can outsmart and outlast her. Andrianova: you beat her with ease, but treat her with respect. Both Benhassi and Catalud if in contention can finish strongly. Watch out for pushing coming in to and during bend. Run economically and keep relaxed as you're doing now. Then, let it go at the right moment. Good luck. Dave*

I was the fastest qualifier, which gives me a good lane draw. I am happy, I am in lane three; normally the top runners are seeded either in three or four to allow them to have a good break.

I head to bed. The hours are ticking away. The 800 metres final, the event I was not even sure I would run in, is so close and I am there in great shape. Only I can let myself down now. I tell myself that is not going to happen. If I run a great race, I have an outside chance of bronze.

Zara, my protective
mother figure

Margo, my coach

Bryan, our team doctor

Pedro, the mad physio

Day Five
Monday, 23 August

IN DREAM WORLD

This is it. Today is finals day.

I know I am in better shape than I have been going into an Olympic Games before and now it is down to me. I won a bronze medal at the last Games and if I win another today, it would be fantastic because I still have, potentially, my main event left: the 1,500 metres. Anything I get out of this race will be a bonus.

I had a relatively good sleep last night. I want to make sure I have another one this afternoon because I am going to feel more tired as I am apprehensive about how it will all go.

I am nervous. At breakfast this morning I had a chat with Ali and Zara. They were telling me to believe in myself. I am going to stick with the same plan but be aware of everyone. The race is at 8.55 p.m. It is only 15 minutes later than the semi-final, so I am not worried about my preparation.

I am lying in my room. I feel like I need to be on my own. I have brought my own laptop computer with me and I have put a DVD on to keep me relaxed. I am watching *Finding Nemo*. Heavy stuff, eh! I am keeping myself to myself, just because I want to conserve as much energy as possible. It is becoming quite hard psychologically. On the one hand I have to give 100 per cent for the 800 metres, trying to leave something for the next day, but I cannot hold back tonight so I have to make sure my recovery plan is on the ball.

Pedro the masseur is at the track when I get there and he starts singing his 'Ring Ring' song to me. He makes me laugh. It keeps me relaxed, though I am quiet. It feels like this race is the be-all and end-all, even though I have hopefully a few more to go later in the week.

I am ready, but I feel slightly different. I can see all the other girls warming up but it is like they are extra people. I do not have any worries about them.

I see Margo over the other side of the track with Jeff. This morning she had been on a run in the village and had come into my room. She wanted to wish me good luck but I could see she felt really awkward about the situation;

she wanted to be with me as much as with Maria. I totally understood that. On the other hand she was my coach and she wanted to give me that guidance. But we never once went through the race, never once went through how she thought I was looking, even though in the back of my mind I thought she kind of saw something different in me and my approach and how I have been racing. Even though she was my coach, I had not told her about my last training session in Cyprus, which was two 400s where I did my personal best time. I needed to keep a little bit of armoury to myself. I kept this training session between Zara, Ali and the British people at the camp and they could not believe how well it went. I knew Margo would never think that I could run that fast. Not because she does not think I have the capability but because she had not seen all the intensity and the work I put in in Cyprus. We had gone through my training plan together but unless you see how the athlete is coping with it, then you do not get a true picture.

Margo told me be strong. Something basic. It was fine. I was happy. My team was there, and that is all I needed: Ali, Zara, Bryan and Bruce. I was grateful that Margo made the effort to come up to me and when I was on the warm-up track, she winked, said good luck and patted me on the back. I knew she was right behind me.

I had played my song a few times during the day but the last occasion before I went out to race I had tears in my eyes. The words had even more relevance to what I was trying to do.

Although I have been an emotional wreck throughout the whole time building up to the Olympics, this was the big moment. I felt something good was going to happen. I do not know why. I have become confident in my ability. This championship felt different to everything else that I have done.

We go to the call room. It is a weird situation. A final is a final but the calibre of people in the race is immense. I have to give it everything I can.

The organisers are getting anxious and irate but I am in such a relaxed mood, nothing will faze me at all. We are taken down to the second call room and I go into the toilet. It is becoming quite a friend.

I put my spikes on and I notice that people are changing their routine and putting spikes on in places where they did not before. For me, everything had to be the same and as soon as anything is different I would be concerned by it. It is the first race where I thought, 'Here we go. Oh my God.'

We go out on to the track. The time is getting nearer. I do my strides, they have gone well. I feel good. Maria runs past, she touches me on the hand, and she says, 'Good luck.' I look for the Union Jack hanging from the top of the stadium. I cannot find it, the wind is blowing a bit, where is it?

I go over my game plan in my mind. I am going to race exactly as I did in the rounds but different people will run the race differently so I have to be aware.

The starting gun fires and I go to the back of the field. Jearl has gone out hard again, with Tatyana following her. They are pushing the pace, the first lap is fast but I remain composed.

Maria and Ceplak are ahead of me and then, along the back straight, the four of us including Behhassi are together.

We pass the bell, we are heading towards the 300-metre mark. I must not go too early. We reach the last 200 metres and the field closes together. I was still far back with 250 metres to go but now I start making my move up. Maria is on my inside and, on the penultimate bend, with 200 metres left, I try to pass her. As I do that, she passes someone else.

I am bumped hard but I deal with it. I could have lost my focus but I have become hardened to it. I come wide off of the top bend and I am level with Maria. We overtake Tatyana and we are going down the home straight together.

We go out on to the track. The time is getting nearer. I do my strides, they have gone well. I feel good.

Being neck and neck with someone is the toughest thing you can do and the fact it is Maria, who I have previously trained with and who I know is strong, makes it that much tougher. In the past, against different people, I have always lost races here. I would always start fighting against myself and race someone else's race. Now all I think about is the line.

The line is getting closer, we are 10 metres away, and I tell myself: relax. I have normally lost it by now, but not this time.

I drop my shoulders like I had practised in training, I use my arms even more but this last 10 metres feels like I am running another 100 metres. It seems so long. Am I there yet? It is only a few strides, it is taking forever.

I cross the line, and people are along side me. Initially I start to celebrate because I know I am first but then reality hits home. How can I have won the Olympic 800 metres final? I think to myself: No. I slowly bring my arms down. If I haven't won it then I am going to look silly celebrating. I am waiting for the replay, I am staring at the giant screen. Ceplak and Benhassi are close to me.

But then a British photographer I know by the side of track, called Michael, yells to me, 'Kelly, you have won.' I can hear him but it does not register. He shouts again. At that moment, I can see I have won and I go mad. My eyes almost pop out of my head. Shall I cry, laugh or scream? I just want someone to run out to pinch me to make me feel it is real.

I am in a daze. I need someone to hug me. It is unbelievable. Will I ever recapture how I feel now?.

I go on a lap of honour. I want to soak up the crowd and the atmosphere and savour this amazing moment. It may never happen again. The crowd are fantastic and the reception I am getting is unbelievable. When I leave the track, the first person I see is Sally and it is all too much. I break down on her shoulder and I cannot speak at all. I do not know what to say. It is just brilliant.

I cannot imagine what my family are thinking about it. I have always been the bridesmaid's bridesmaid but I knew I could never give up. There was always something inside me that said I can do it. I was right.

I go alongside the mixed zone and I am interviewed by television stations from Germany, Australia, France and Japan. I do not even know if I am making sense.

I want to see Ali and Zara. They have been on this whole emotional journey with me. I speak to the journalists from the British press and I don't think they expected me to win. No one, including myself, did.

People are asking what is it like to be Olympic champion. OK, enough is enough, pinch me, wake me up, the race has not even started yet. How do I answer these sort of questions, because in the back of my mind is the thought of how would I run tomorrow?

It is time for the presentation. I am in a complete daze. Bryan English is there with Philip Pope, the media officer from the British Olympic Association,

and then Lord Sebastian Coe comes over. At this stage I am shaking like a leaf. Seb gives me a big hug and says what a brilliant race I had run and if only he had run like that in his Olympic quest. What an honour: my hero, one of the legends of the sporting world, and he is congratulating me!

The medal ceremony is delayed because there is a small inquiry about the second and third positions. I wasn't aware of what was happening but Jolanda Ceplak had tried to see if the officials were sure she was in third behind Hasna Benhassi. Maria finished fourth in the end. That is the worst position to finish in the Olympics. I feel for her. I don't blame Jolanda for wanting to check, because both athletes were given the same time as each other of 1:56.43. I won in 1:56.38. During the delay, Seb is still talking to me as I am pacing up and down in the tunnel which leads on to the track to where the podium is. I can see the British flags flying and I just can't believe it.

Any time now I will be going out there to receive my gold medal. The thought scares me. As I stand for a few seconds, Seb says, 'Why don't you do your cool down?' Suddenly the realisation of the fact that I have to be back here tomorrow for the heats of the 1,500 metres hits me! I say, 'Yes, I'd better!' Then the legend of athletics crouches down on his knees and starts to undo the laces of my spikes – can you believe it? Seb Coe helping me, Kelly Holmes, to get my shoes off! This was becoming more surreal by the second! The reason we do a cool down is to get rid of any lactic acid (which is soreness of the muscles and causes them to stiffen up). The shakes continue as I get ready. The inquiry is still going on but I ask Jolanda if she fancies joining me. She does. I was really pleased that Jolanda had won a medal because I could see how much she wanted it and she has run so well this year.

I spot Bruce. I have to be ready for the 1,500 metres tomorrow and I ask him if he will give me an ice rub. Dean Kenneally, UK Athletics head physiotherapist, is there too and they both help me out. The UK Athletics medical team has been fantastic at these Games. As an athlete you know that you can rely on their support 100 per cent. As we are about to finish, one of the ladies in charge of the ceremony comes running in. 'It is time to get your medal,' she says.

This is it: here I go, it's really going to happen. I had kept the flag I was given on my lap of honour, so I decide to drape this around my waist like a sarong. Jolanda and Hasna do the same with their national flags. It's funny that, when you race, everyone is your rival, but when you come to receive a medal at a major championship all that is totally forgotten. We are lined up in order: second, first, and third. I hear the fanfare music for the medal ceremony. We walk out into the stadium and a huge cheer goes up. I know it is the Brits – they are always so good at getting behind us athletes and I know that thousands of them are with me now.

Jolanda was third, Hasna was second. They are given flowers and olive wreath crowns, and then it is my turn. The announcer says, 'And Olympic Champion for 800 metres in Athens 2004 is … Kelly Holmes.' I go on to the podium to what is a deafening roar from the crowd. I don't know whether to smile, laugh or cry, but I want to savour this moment for as long as I can.

I am presented with my medal by none other than Seb. I still have visions of him undoing my laces! The significance of the fact that Lord Sebastian Coe was presenting me with my medal is another moment I will never ever forget. We turn right to face the flag masts and the tannoy announces the national anthem of Great Britain to yet another massive cheer from the crowd. As 'God Save The Queen' starts to blast out around the stadium, and the flags start to rise, the hairs on the back of my neck stand up. You never think something like this will become reality. It is something I have dreamed of, probably every night of my athletics career.

The British flag rises in between the Slovenian and Moroccan ones. Again it hits home: I am the champion. As the national anthem goes into full flow, it sounds like everyone in the crowd is singing along – they are! I try to sing but all I can do is stare at my flag and look around the vast stadium at all the proud British fans that were enjoying this special moment with me. The national anthem finishes to extraordinary cheers. The crowd starts chanting my name. I wave to them all, still in a daze full of excitement and disbelief.

The obligatory photo call follows. The atmosphere is out of this world. I go straight to a press conference, sitting on a top table alongside Ceplak and Benhassi (who has an interpreter). I am asked questions such as: How do I feel? Did I think I could win before the race? I can hardly answer, I just don't know how to take in the feeling, all I can really do is keep repeating in my head that I have finally done it. As I am sitting there, the race is a bit of blur. I think I am still in shock (maybe as much as the now famous photo, which at this time was being printed all over the world, shows – the one with my eyes popping out of my head!). For some reason as all these questions are being fired at me I have this feeling of peace surrounding me.

Someone asks me if I believed I would win. 'I knew I was in great shape,' I reply, 'but win? Never in a million years. Look who I was up against!' But deep down I know the answer is yes.

The written press don't normally show much emotion; they're usually firing direct questions at me, looking for that extra twist to their story,

43

especially if they have nothing better to write – but this time is different, there is none of that. They seem genuinely happy for me and, as most of them have followed me along my rollercoaster journey, this was the end of a massive long climb.

The press conference finishes and I am whisked off to doping control. At these Olympics it is compulsory for the first four placed athletes in every final to be given a blood and urine test. I am very happy to have to have it; the only annoyance is that after racing you normally can't go to the loo for ages, and also knowing that I still have to be back here for tomorrow night's race. I am really hoping that I won't have to spend what usually takes me two hours waiting to give a sample. Bryan is with me in doping control and does his best to see if I can get the blood test done tonight because I am racing tomorrow. It is the last distraction I need. But rules are rules. I book in for 11 a.m. the following day and under no circumstances can I be late. After eventually giving my urine sample it is time to go. I only take an hour – result!

A few more interviews, but they are kept to a minimum and I agree to do the BBC next morning in the village after Zara has got Max Jones, our head coach, to call the BOA and say I don't want to do it that night because I am shattered – a good move!

I am taken back to the village in a car and finally get to the small dining hall where I see Zara, then Ali. I give them both a massive hug and they are so excited and extremely pleased for me. Zara has been like a mother to me in Athens – the nagging type of course! And she is straight into giving me my instructions for the night … ice bath, nightmare! It is 12.30 a.m. and I hate the cold, but of course I know she is right.

Jo Pavey is also down there and that makes me feel better. She has just run a fantastic race to finish fifth in the 5,000 metres and she too is going to be racing in the 1,500 metres heat the next day and that actually makes it a bit easier for me to deal with, knowing someone else has the same 'Do I have to?' thoughts going through their head!

The night is now at an end. It has been amazing but it doesn't make me a better person than anyone else. I am still Kelly and I will always be the same Kelly that people know me as now. Why would I change?

I am in my room. I sit on the end of my bed and stare at my medal. Tears fill my eyes and that is the first time I have cried since winning. I am on my own and it hits me for real that I am the Olympic Champion. **,**

The night is now at an end. It has been amazing but it doesn't make me a better person than anyone else.

45

Day Six
Tuesday, 24 August

AND FOR MY NEXT TRICK

It is morning. I wake up still in disbelief. I have the medal on the pillow next to me and I am staring it. Gold from the 800 metres; just a few days ago I was undecided about even running this distance and now I am the Olympic champion. But it is time to focus on what is going to be another long day. I could lie here all day I suppose, just thinking back to last night. Did it happen? Did it really happen? An entry in my diary that now says 'Kelly Holmes, Olympic 800 metres champion'.

How did that happen? Well, it happened because I must have some will power that I am not quite sure about, a determination that nothing will break me. Often, during all those times of pain and injuries, I thought about quitting. I said to myself back in 1999 that if I had one more major problem, that would be it. I had that problem but I carried on. I always knew that if I could just go for a season free from trouble, maybe, just maybe, I could do it.

It would be foolish of me to think I am going to stroll through the day, then arrive at the track and win the first heat of the 1,500 metres like it was a one-off. It is the opening round and I would like to think I have enough strength to qualify OK but I am taking nothing for granted. How will my body react? Now comes the big test. I am feeling so good in terms of having no injuries; I only hope I do not get affected by something because of what is going to be a punishing schedule.

I do not race until 8.38 p.m., but I am feeling tired already. Focus, Kelly!

What is amazing is that originally I was coming here to run only the 1,500 metres. That distance was always my main event for the year. I would like to think that if everything fits into place I will be good for a medal in Saturday night's final, but those four days seem a long way away.

I feel like I did on the first day of the 800 metre heats. I am beginning to wonder if I can actually run this first 1,500 metres; it is always good to get the first one out of the way.

AUGUST 19
AUGUST 20
AUGUST 21
AUGUST 22
AUGUST 23
AUGUST 24
AUGUST 25
AUGUST 26
AUGUST 27
AUGUST 28
1
2
3
4
5
6
7
8
9
10

I'm booked in to see Ali later this morning but first I have to do my interview with the BBC that was arranged last night. The BOA has a press media area set up with television links in the village. It makes life so much easier, because the last thing I want to do at nine in the morning is to start travelling somewhere.

I wander across. Everyone is smiling, the congratulations have started again and it is fantastic. I am miked up and I am on air. I am introduced as an Olympic champion! I am asked questions about my race the night before and everyone is saying how brilliantly I have done and how all the commentators lost their sense of professionalism as their pride and excitement took over with them screaming for me to win.

The interview goes well. Suddenly there is another special moment. Ann Packer, the last British woman to win Olympic gold in the 800 metres, back in 1964, is speaking to me live from the UK. It is bizarre. I had seen so many pictures of her crossing the line in that race in Tokyo and remember reading about it. I often wondered if I could achieve what she did and now I have.

It is 11 a.m. We are at the doping control centre in the village where I am having my blood test. I am on time (for once in my life) and Bryan is with me. The blood test consists of four tubes; two are then spun in a machine so that the blood and the plasma separate. Eventually the tubes are sealed and sent off to the laboratory to be tested for various performance-enhancing drugs and I head back for my last 'duty' of the day. It is another media interview, this time with my old friend Colin Jackson.

We are now back in the village, in the media area on top of a roof. The sun is shining, there seems a buzz around the place and around my neck I have a gold medal. I cannot stop touching it, feeling it. Perhaps just to convince myself that it is true.

I like doing interviews with Colin. We have a laugh. As we meet up, he starts screaming and staring at me and saying, 'You've gone and done it!'

The interview goes well and now it is time for lunch. Today I'm having pasta and salad because, as I am tired, I am not that hungry, but I know I have to eat to maintain my energy for tonight's race.

I have some treatment from Ali. It is painful, every muscle in my body is stiff, probably because I ran the second fastest time of my life yesterday and my usual warm-down routine had not been the best. Ali sorts out my legs, ankles and back. I felt quite battered beforehand and Ali's massages are pain not pleasure. My back was tense and in the past it has affected my

'While watching Kelly come down that home straight, I'm no religious man, but believe me I was praying, screaming for her! When she crossed that line first my eyes welled up I was so emotional and that was just the 800!'
Colin Jackson, CBE

breathing. She decides to give me acupuncture, with needles placed into the tight area to relax the muscles. It sounds nasty but, believe me, it is less pain than Ali's elbows.

At last, time to relax. I feel quite stressed by now because I know I have to race and my preparation has not been good. I am back in my room. It is mid-afternoon. I look at my medal. I smile and think: whatever is meant to happen tonight, will happen. I take half a sleeping tablet. I wouldn't normally do that before a race but if I don't have an hour, at least, for my body to shut off I will not be able to perform. I figure out that I will probably run well in a relaxed state rather than if I am exhausted. As I go to bed, I play my song again and the tears start flowing…

When I wake up, I feel focused on what I need to do tonight. The qualifying requirements to progress through are the first five in each heat with the nine fastest losers. I hope I will be OK.

I leave for the track about two-and-a-half hours before the race, on the bus with Zara. I am a bit subdued, because I wasn't able to celebrate my previous night's win and it is back to business immediately.

When I reach the warm-up track, Jo Pavey and Hayley Tullett, the other British entries for the 1,500 metres, are already there. We are not in the same heat and I am sure, like me, they are hoping for the best for each other.

My warm-up procedure is exactly the same as for the 800 metres, except that this time Margo, my coach, is at the track. She is able to be part of my team because Maria (Mutola) is not running the 1,500 metres, but the funny thing is that I can tell how protective Zara is in not wanting us to change my routine at this stage. Margo understands what is going on. She is just relieved that there is no conflict of interest and she can now root for me all the way.

The preparation for the race is exactly the same as the other races but something has changed. My lucky dog tag was stolen from my bag last night. I am wearing a new one that the kit man, Charlie, who we call Charlie Farley, gave me. It does not actually worry me because I think, a new start for a new day.

As I am feeling tired, I plan the best way for me to get through this race in the most comfortable fashion. And, because my tactics of staying at the back had worked so well in the 800 metres, I decide to do the same again. It is a longer race but I have grown in confidence from my ability to perform so well in the 800 metres.

I go through the same procedure in the call-up room and then I am back in the Olympic Stadium where, 24 hours earlier, I had become the Olympic champion.

The whole race goes by in a blur. All I can remember is feeling tired. But I come up on the outside, doing just enough to qualify by finishing second in 4:05.58 behind Natalya Yevdokimova of Russia, who wins in 4:05.55.

I head to Sally. She gives me cashew nuts this time and I munch them quite contentedly as I stand with her doing an interview. The media are a bit more full-on tonight and all the television stations now want to talk to not only an Olympic champion, but one that potentially has the chance of medalling in her favourite event.

I keep the interviews to a minimum. I go straight back to the recovery procedure and, on cue, Bryan appears with my rehydration energy bag.

I am proud of myself in the way I have been able to maintain this precise programme after racing for so many years but it is all down to Zara and Ali.

When I get back to the village, all I want to do is go to bed. I eat first and then have an ice bath and, thankfully, tomorrow is a rest day. I head to my room. I lay the medal beside me; I am tired tonight. Even Olympic champions need their rest, I suppose.

Day Seven
Wednesday, 25 August

LEAVE ME ALONE, I AM ON A GO SLOW!

At last, a rest day and am I enjoying this. No one will ever know what it means to me. I am not going to allow anything to distract me from rest. It has been crazy. But I am not doing any interviews. I have made it through to the semi-finals and now I am going to ease my way towards tomorrow night's race without any stress. I do not have to focus on racing for once and it benefits me no end. My priority is to get my body checked over with Ali but also to get a new hairdo. My hair has become a major talking point within the athletics team. I had it done in Cyprus, braided by a British hairdresser called Patricia, and everyone in the team seems to have latched on to the fact that I keep wanting more done to it.

I need to get out of the camp. I need some breathing space. Along with Kate Howey, the Olympic judo silver medallist from Sydney, and Lorraine Shaw, the Commonwealth hammer-throwing champion, I leave the village.

We are at the British Lodge, the area where families can meet team members, and we relax by the pool. It gives me the chance to forget about my race. I have become quite stressed about it all and I find it hard to maintain my concentration. I have to, though, because Zara is constantly reminding me that this was the race that I had done all this hard and intense training for, not the 800 metres.

The day has gone quickly. Typical. You hope it will last for a long time but, before you know it, you are back in the village having dinner. Jo Pavey and I normally laugh that the things we do best are eat and sleep – but it could not be further from the truth this time.

I have been on a random kit hunt because I keep forgetting to collect my stuff from the launderette. I need more crop tops. I find David Dix, the UK Athletics administrator, and he helps me out.

It is night time. The diary is short and sweet today because it has gone as planned – nothing has happened. I look at my medal. I give it a long kiss. I am determined to have a good night's sleep.

53

Day Eight
Thursday, 26 August

TWO TO GO

I wake up ready and I feel good today. The hard training in Cyprus that I did with the help of Anthony Whiteman is paying off. Over there, in a short space of time, I went through a great deal of training and back-to-back sessions, and he helped me out with pace-making which makes it much easier for me to motivate myself.

Zara has the semi-final lists. She has told me who is in the race. I do not want to look at them in much depth because I have decided it is not what I need to see. As long as I know what the qualifying is, who I have to watch out for, and the amount of people who might make it difficult for me to qualify, then that is it. Like in the 800 metres semi-final, I have a tough draw, with Olga Yegorova of Russia in my race. It is the first five from each heat who qualify, plus the two fastest losers from the two semi-finals, so I am hopeful that I will make it through.

I take it pretty easy. I do not want to do much because it is a crucial day and I am feeling pretty nervous. I keep myself to myself. I play my song four times, along with other music, and I see Ali because my back is still stiff and she does some more work on it.

It is time to go. Zara meets me to walk to the bus at the top of the village. I want to really focus. I feel a bit under pressure myself, just wanting to get through the day, and I do not know the pressure that is building up back home.

In the first round of the 1,500 metres I had not thought about the race that much, because I was happy from the night before having won gold and the qualification seemed quite easy. I am more nervous for this one, maybe because the girls who are in the race are quality 1,500 metre runners, whereas I go between the two, 800 metres and 1,500 metres. I am not sure how my legs will be.

AUGUST 19
AUGUST 20
AUGUST 21
AUGUST 22
AUGUST 23
AUGUST 24
AUGUST 25
AUGUST 26
AUGUST 27
AUGUST 28

1
2
3
4
5
6
7
8
9
10

We arrive at the track. My warm-up is fine. Margo meets me and she says, 'Run as you normally do. You are looking great; hang back for the first two laps.' I decide that is the best thing to carry on doing.

I do my warm ups, the same routine as usual, and I can tell Zara is wanting to make sure I keep my focus at all times, but she is happy that Margo is there and involved in my preparation this time. Zara likes the fact that she can be in control of what we are doing and she also makes a point of telling me how long it is until we have to go to the call-up room. I can tell that she just wants to be there with me; after all she has been there in Cyprus and through the whole 800 metres experience. She wants to keep me in that same routine. I am happy that Margo is here to see me perform and to be part of the moment, but Zara is the one who is keeping me going.

I am on the track and I can hear all the British fans shouting my name, but I remain very focused. I do not react to the crowd at all. It is not time to celebrate any more but to regroup my thoughts on what I am there to achieve. I know I am capable of reaching the final and doing something really good and the only person who can mess up that is me.

I am standing on the start line and they announce me as 'Kelly Holmes, the 800 metre Olympic champion', and that is pretty amazing. It is weird when it happens. It is me they are talking about.

I am ready to run. I have to make sure I am in a good position to qualify.

I stay at the back for the first 800 metres. I feel that, if I am relaxed, I will be saving my energy. I am not sure if my legs will feel tired in the heats. Running even laps is my best way to get through. I know I am strong. I gradually make my way up the field. I need to be in fifth position to qualify and I always make sure I am close enough to the fifth person, so that if the worst comes to the worst I can always sprint past her to ensure I make it.

I am doing much better than I thought I was going to do. The day off has done me wonders and the back-to-back training sessions I have done in the past are proving beneficial considering the amount of races I have run in the Games.

I am in contention along the home straight. I glance over to the left, mainly to count how many people are there. Shall I overtake these people? Zara and Margo say don't show everything you have got. I go past four but decide to hang back and show nothing.

I finish second. I am in the final.

I see Sally, who has my nuts as usual. We have a chat, I progress through the mixed zone and it is weird because normally at these championships you always talk to the odd television crew from abroad, maybe Australia because of the British interest over there. But this time everyone wants to speak to me, including Japanese television. It has become a big thing that the Olympic champion is still racing and is now in a second final.

I keep composed. Everyone wants to talk to me but I am aware I have to do my warm downs and that tomorrow is a rest day. The more I can recover from this race, the more I can have a happy rest day. I am asked that, now I am in the final of the 1,500 metres, had I thought that if I won I would go down in history by achieving something that Coe and Ovett never did. I haven't, because I did not think it would happen in the first place; I did not think I would win the 800 metres.

I need the rest day tomorrow. My body is being taken to its maximum, it is not going to last forever and I better make the most of it. I don't do a lot with Ali because I know I can see her the next day.

I am tired but not too tired. You become tired from getting yourself up for the warm-up and warm-down. You do not realise it as you are using all that adrenaline.

I have dinner, and an ice bath. I see Jo Pavey who unfortunately has not got through. I go to bed.

Day Nine
Friday, 27 August

A GOOD HAIR DAY

Today is another rest day and I am looking forward to relaxing as much as possible. I am not wearing my medal all the time. Although I look at it every morning, and have that tear in my eye because of what I have achieved, as I am still running the 1,500 metres I do not want it to be the most prominent thing around.

It is really hard to do, hard to try to forget almost. I attempt to block it out as much as possible. I keep the medal locked in my room and I am able to make myself think that the 1,500 metres is the start of my championship and that mindset is what helps get me through.

I have one more race to go at these Olympics. It has been a long and drawn-out experience and I have to keep my focus. Zara is drumming in to me every time I see her that the 1,500 metres is the event that I have been training for and this is the one that I want to win. I keep telling her that I have already done one. But she says, 'No, the 1,500 metres is what you have been aiming for all year' and tells me that I cannot relax too much because there is only one race to go.

Since the 1,500 metres started, I have said to Ali pretty much every day: 'Do I have to run, do I have to go out there?' It is more a reassurance thing. I need that extra bit of confidence to keep going and Ali would always reply: 'Look, your body is in brilliant shape, you are in the best form of your life. It's only one more race, two more days and you have finished – just keep the focus for that bit longer.' Whenever I see Zara and Ali I say the bit about 'Do I have to run?', just wanting them to keep telling me that everything will be fine and I can do it'. Even though now I know I cannot give in. I believe I will never be in this shape in my life again because I will not be able to have this amount of focus and commitment to what I have done.

While I am in this shape, I have to keep it going as much as possible. I am doing the normal things today. Ali has checked everything over, it is all pretty good. My back was tight so she did the acupuncture again.

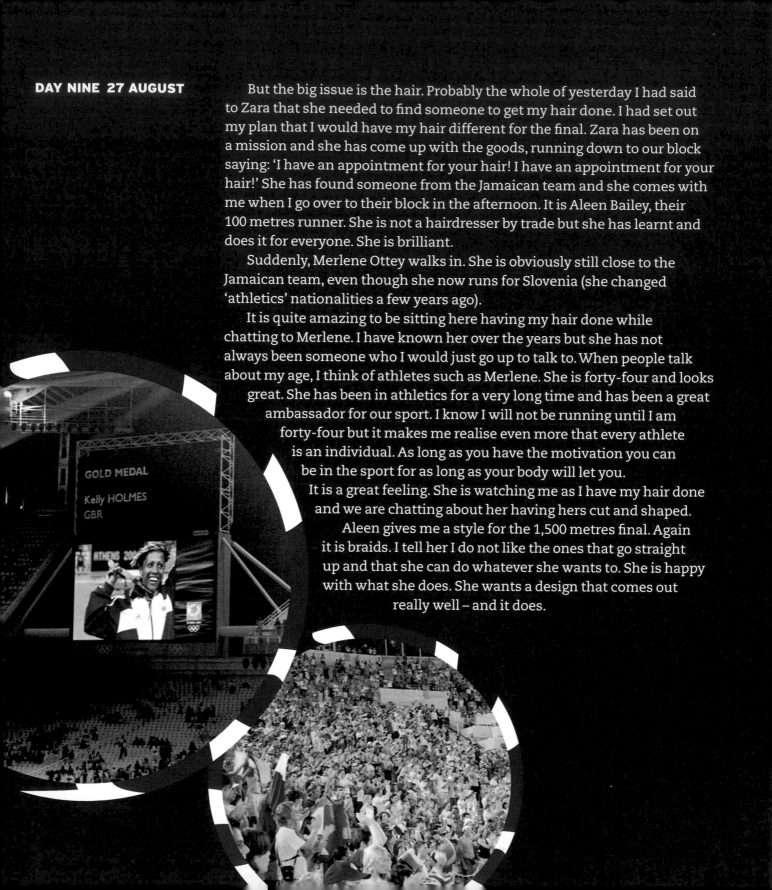

DAY NINE 27 AUGUST

But the big issue is the hair. Probably the whole of yesterday I had said to Zara that she needed to find someone to get my hair done. I had set out my plan that I would have my hair different for the final. Zara has been on a mission and she has come up with the goods, running down to our block saying: 'I have an appointment for your hair! I have an appointment for your hair!' She has found someone from the Jamaican team and she comes with me when I go over to their block in the afternoon. It is Aleen Bailey, their 100 metres runner. She is not a hairdresser by trade but she has learnt and does it for everyone. She is brilliant.

Suddenly, Merlene Ottey walks in. She is obviously still close to the Jamaican team, even though she now runs for Slovenia (she changed 'athletics' nationalities a few years ago).

It is quite amazing to be sitting here having my hair done while chatting to Merlene. I have known her over the years but she has not always been someone who I would just go up to talk to. When people talk about my age, I think of athletes such as Merlene. She is forty-four and looks great. She has been in athletics for a very long time and has been a great ambassador for our sport. I know I will not be running until I am forty-four but it makes me realise even more that every athlete is an individual. As long as you have the motivation you can be in the sport for as long as your body will let you.

It is a great feeling. She is watching me as I have my hair done and we are chatting about her having hers cut and shaped. Aleen gives me a style for the 1,500 metres final. Again it is braids. I tell her I do not like the ones that go straight up and that she can do whatever she wants to. She is happy with what she does. She wants a design that comes out really well – and it does.

GOLD MEDAL

Kelly HOLMES
GBR

It is a big night for her. It is the final of the 4 x 100 metres relay. I was very conscious of that and I had asked Zara beforehand if it was OK. But Aleen wanted to do it – it would take her mind off the fact that she was in the final.

A significant thing happens. She says, 'I cannot believe I am doing the hair of an Olympic champion and if I touch it, maybe it will give us good luck for tonight and maybe we can come back with gold'. Little did I know what they would do – that was weird, all these moments of fate surrounding me. When she is on her lap of honour with the rest of her team mates, I remember what she had said a few hours earlier and that it has come true. Not that I am saying my hair had given them the ability to win – just that sentence!

As she does my hair, we are talking about where she will run next. I figure that I will probably be able to catch up with her somewhere else and it will mean I would not have all this panic about trying to find someone to do my hair every time. She tells me her last few races and that she is going to the same ones that I am (she ends up doing my hair for the World Athletics Final in Monaco). She wants nothing for doing it. Later Zara gets loads of the British kit to give to her as a thank you. She is really grateful for it.

Aleen is really quick, about an hour and has done this fantastic pattern. It is amazing to see how these girls braid hair. Along with my 'beach lady,' Patricia, who I met while training in Cyprus, they are the key people for my hair. They have the gold and silver medals. It is very close, I cannot separate which one would get which!

I leave with Zara. I want to remain relaxed today. I go to the international zone for a look around. There are a few shops there, a photo shop, banks, a mobile phone place and a general store to buy gifts. There is not a lot to do but I sit down and have an orange juice, watching loads of different people going by. I relax. A couple of athletes from different countries come up and chat with me.

I go back down to my block. I sleep well that night. I was tired but I was wary that I had to have a great night's sleep before the final. It would be a big day; it would take a lot out of me. '

Day Ten
Saturday, 28 August

MY CHANCE TO BECOME A LEGEND

It is 7.00 a.m. and I have woken up early again. I am lying in bed, playing some music. I have not been sleeping well throughout the whole championships because I have so much on my mind, with all the adrenaline and emotions running through me.

It is breakfast as normal in my apartment. I have not gone over to the canteen for breakfast because I can have it when I want it and get up when I want to – and relax.

Margo has called me to see when she can come over to have a chat about the final. I do not normally like to talk about my races on the day but I did not want to speak about the final yesterday. That was my rest day; I wanted it out of my mind.

Margo has gone with Zara to look at the footage from the semi-finals from Thursday to see who are the key people to watch out for tonight. I did not want to go up there because at the end of the day I am in great shape and only I can control what I do. I need to know who the major people in contention are and I will only get it from someone else telling me as I am not aware of what happened in the other races.

It is late morning. Margo is here and we are going through the plan. We are in my room. We are chatting about how I will run and what my best chances are of doing well. At this stage Margo definitely thinks I am in line to do something big. The other girls are big threats because they are all fantastic 1,500 metres runners. We discuss my game plan. We talk about the whole race and where I should be at what stage and when I should make a move up the field. If it is a slow race it will be to my advantage because I am definitely the fastest runner over the shorter distance and possibly the rest of the girls will pull the pace along.

We assume the pace will be quite quick and I will have to be more aware of my position and not become detached from the field. We decide I will stay pretty much at the back for the first 800 metres and not even think about

63

moving up. After that point I will progress a couple of places, towards the bell I will be in about fifth or sixth place and move up a little further so I am in total contention with about 200 metres left. Then I will be able to kick when I want to.

It is always good to go into a race with an idea of how you would like to run and maybe you have two or three game plans. I am confident enough to know that if the plan does not work out I have the experience to counter it.

We talk about the other runners: Tomashova; Cioncan, who has a strong finish; Benhassi, who is in the race having finished second in the 800 metres and has an amazing finish; and then there are all the Russian and Polish athletes. The 1,500 metres is a tough field. We have had a good chat. Margo has been with me more for the 1,500 metres but did not want to mess around with my preparation. I think she felt a bit strange as she was not able to be with me for the 800 metres when I did what I did.

The final is a different matter. You want to get as much information as possible and that is really where Margo helped to do that. Since being with Margo my mindset for training has changed a lot and I love having her as my coach.

After our chat we go to lunch at the small dining hall. Agnes joins us. It is nice and relaxing and then Ali, Zara and a few others come up a bit later. I am not thinking about the race. At lunch we talk about normal things. I am not too hungry because I am a bit nervous, so close to the final.

After lunch, I go to get my laundry. I had sent Christian Malcolm to collect it the other day – he is so nice. Ali then checks me to make sure everything is right and she gives me the reassurance to go for it that night.

I remember walking back down to my apartment and meeting Max Jones. He tells me what I have done has made me one of the greatest athletes but if I win the final of the 1,500 metres, it will make me a legend.

I cannot really get my head around what he is saying. Things had been going so well but I never dreamt this would happen.

I go back to my room to chill for the rest of the afternoon. The race is at 8.30 p.m. We leave at about 5.50 p.m. to walk to the first bus. We have to get an internal bus in the camp that drops us off at the international zone. Coaches have been parked there for all the different sports. We are now near the end of the Olympics and there are only a few buses around for other sports because most of the events have finished. But it is the final day of the athletics and there are quite a few buses put on for that because many people who have finished competing are going down to watch. It is a bit different. Ali and a couple of other people come down with us. In a way this is a bit weird. Every day I had been travelling with Zara and we had been leaving on our own – the same routine and I will see Ali at the track. Now she is with us. I want her to come down, obviously, but inside I am thinking it has changed the routine. I do not know if that is a good thing. I wonder if everything will change.

I am a bit weary. It is only a bus ride. I am being superstitious and I do not want anything to go wrong. When I lost my dog tag, I said that is like the start of a new event. Now I am picking up on any little thing that is happening.

Then we arrive at the track and the physios have moved also. It is the first time they have done that and I think: everything is different.

I am not upset in a bad way and I say to Ali 'We are not allowed to be here, we have to be down the bottom.' But everyone has already set up. She is trying to keep me calm but I tell her things can't change. Another team had set up down there and I think: It is only a position on the track but I feel a bit superstitious.

I decide to lie down to close my eyes for a bit. There are many people at the track. It is the final day and the relays are going on.

A bit later our men's 4 x 100 metres sprint team are here, they are milling around and they seem to be up for it. They are all wearing the same kit and looking the part, not just as individuals coming together for a relay. I watch them practice and think to myself that it is one of the first times in a while that they are all getting on really well, all having a good laugh, and there does not seem to be any of that atmosphere that normally surrounds the sprinters.

Ali looks at my ankles, checking to make sure everything is OK. Much of it is in my head now because I am expecting something to go wrong because it has been so perfect for me, then with the change of the bus ride, I worry that something is not going to go right. I have become a bit paranoid.

I see Pedro, our masseur. He is a long-haired guy from Cyprus and is full of energy with a wicked sense of humour and he has been significant during this week because he would make me laugh and I need that. Even if it is only for a few seconds, it would take my mind off of what I was doing. He comes up to me as I am getting ready for this race and I ask him to sing our 'Ring Ring' song. He does, it makes me laugh, as usual, and it is good for me.

I begin my warm up, same routine as normal. I feel really relaxed. I am nervous inside but it is more like apprehension. It is my last race and I might as well make it a good one.

I remember at the Olympics in Sydney in 2000 that by the time of the 1,500 metres final I had lost my focus. I did not have the support structure that I needed. I did have people around me, my old coach Dave (Arnold), but I was so happy to have won the 800 metres bronze medal, that I was in the 1,500 metres just to run. This time it is totally different. I am Olympic champion. I have to stay focused.

Surprisingly my legs feel really good after my warm up. I have the spring back from the earlier days. My song is in my head and I then sing it out loud but no one is listening!

Tonight they are playing more music over the tannoy. I sing along to some of their songs, and then have my song back in my head.

The other girls in the race are warming up but it does not faze me. Margo comes with me when I do my stretching and drills on the top track. They go well.

It is busy tonight; something else that is different. I hope these things are changing to keep my mind off things rather than be a complete distraction on the last race.

I do my strides as normal. I put my spikes on and do some sprints. I feel good.

The relay guys are jogging around with the baton. They are looking confident. I am thinking 'Good on you!' I have a feeling something is going to happen tonight.

Margo tells me I look really strong – that I should believe in myself and run to my plan.

It is time to go. Margo has given me that talk and now Zara takes over as we go to the first call room for the final time. I keep thinking to myself that everything I am doing is for the last time at these Games: my drills, my strides and my journey to the call room.

The 1,500 metres girls are not as friendly as the 800 metres. You do not really acknowledge many people when you are racing but in the 800 metres there is always someone who I mouth 'Good luck' to. It is only brief but it does not happen in the 1,500 metres. It is quiet. I do not think about the people in the race – just that these are the people I have to beat. There is a former world champion here and a couple of runners who had beaten me earlier in the season but I do not make a big point of the fact they are here. It is the first time I have seen exactly who is in the whole field. I have been told who the main people are but I am not aware of who make up the final twelve. There is nothing I can do. I have to race against them.

We walk down a little slope where we get to the track for the final warm-up area. There is a camera following me around but not imposing on my space. I suppose I am one of the news stories of these Games (I did not realise how much until after them but I know now).

All the girls drop their bags and they go to do their strides. I put my spikes on and think: I will do mine on the track. I am happy. I am keeping to my plan. We are called out on to the track. I kiss my lucky charm. The cameraman follows me. Then from that moment on, I just focus on the race.

I do not feel as nervous as in the semi-final. All I can do is what I do, I cannot control what other people do in the race. I remember that the Jamaican women were receiving their medals for winning the 4 x 100 metres relay and the thought comes into my head of what Aleen had said – and it kind of makes me smile. It is strange how now this is happening and I am going to run my final.

It is time for the race. I am not put off by anything around me. It is like a buzz. There is cheering and the odd name being called out–mine quite a bit by the British supporters. I am not distracted. It is the start of the race that will make history for Britain.

The gun goes and I head towards the back. I keep exactly to the plan – I will not do anything for the first 800 metres. I am not aware of anyone in the race except Benhassi. I remember her straight away going behind me. She has a really fast finish and I keep it in my head that she is there. I have no clue who is leading or who I am behind; all I remember is being at the back.

The discussions I had with Margo come into play, certain places I will move. (While I am running like this, I was later told that Margo was in the stadium with Ali, Bryan and that she was saying: stay at the back, and I was at the back; move up two places, and I moved up two places; get into fifth place, I went into fifth place. Bryan said it was like I had a little earpiece and she was telling me what to do and I was doing it.)

I am not aware of the clock during the race; not even of the lap counter. But I know how many I have done – and how many there are to go.

I am caught by someone, it does not affect me, just like in the 800 metres. I stick my left arm out and push them back and carry on running.

All I know is where I want to be in that race no matter what and anyone who is in my way will soon be out of it!

I am back into my position. I make a significant move down the back straight. I want to be in contention in that final 150 metres. I come around the top bend. I look around. (People asked me later why I did that. The reason was Benhassi.

She had been behind me but I had not seen her for the whole race.) I think to myself, I must check where she is. I look to both sides. I cannot see her, she is off the pace, I have to make sure because once I make my move that is it, there is nothing left in the tank. There is no one close to me with a better kick than mine and with 90 metres left, I make my move. But not 100 per cent.

Then I put in a second kick with 50 metres to go. I open up and the feeling when I cross the line is indescribable.

I have won this, the one I wanted to. But to think I have my second gold… there are no words to sum up how I feel. I throw my arms up. This time my eyes are closed, I do that on purpose! My mouth is open. I could not believe I had won the 800 metres. I know I have won the 1,500 metres. The realisation I have my second gold is unbelievable. My time is 3:57.90, a British record.

I go crazy. The adrenaline takes over me. I am so excited. But I am so tired straightaway from the energy I have used in the race. It is like every last bit of energy I could find has been put into it.

I go onto my knees, mainly because I am tired, also because I cannot believe it.

'Oh my God , oh my God, I have won it, I have won.' I even cry a bit. I am overcome by it all; sheer relief and everything comes out. I feel totally exhausted.

I get up. I have tears in my eyes and the crowd are going mad.

I put my hands over my face. What have I done!

It is unbelievable.

A huge amount of photographers are in front of me; they are going crazy.

It is the lap of honour. I get another British flag, soaking up the atmosphere but I can hardly walk, let alone jog. I start to, but my legs have totally gone.

All the British flags are flying and it is amazing.

I take it all in.

A buggy with a television crew on it is ahead of me. I manage to lift my arms up on a few occasions with the flag but I cannot do it for long. I am so tired. The lap of honour ends. I see Sally, who gives me a massive hug and as I am standing waiting to be interviewed by her, other journalists are shouting at me. I chat to her for ages. She gives me nuts again. I have so many cashews! It is so cool but in a way this time I do not need them because I am not running again. I say hello to everyone at home, I hope they were enjoying it all – but I am probably talking loads of waffle as usual.

You can imagine. I do every single television channel. I am saying hello to every screen of every channel – I am so happy. I am probably not even speaking to the interviewer!

But behind the smiles I am in real pain. Throughout the years I have suffered with an extremely bad tearing sensation in the lower part of my stomach and it has started again. All the medics are aware of it.

Bryan is there and he sees me. He tells me that before I finish off seeing the media we have to go under the stands – where he gives me a pain-killing injection. It is pitch black. Not exactly a luxury thing for a double Olympic champion to see, this dark, dirty area. But my stomach is killing me. The press never know that this happens to me. Normally I say I have to go quickly – and I have a muscle relaxing injection or painkiller, depending how bad it is. Bryan started helping me a year or two ago. I would be in so much agony, I would be delirious, and sometimes be sick.

I then crawl out of this area under the stand. It is a weird moment again. People do not know about this background stuff. One minute I am elated on television and then the next – pain. I have the injection and come out smiling again after dying under there for five or ten minutes and carry on like nothing has happened.

DAY TEN 28 AUGUST

Next I go to BBC Radio Five where Sonia McLaughlin (their interviewer) and Matt Allen (their producer) are there and they are well excited for me.

I put on some headphones. I can hear my mum. She is on the line and obviously she is so happy. She is asked what she is going to say to me when she speaks to me. She replies: 'Well, what can you say to someone who has achieved her dream'. She does not know I am on the other end of the line. I speak to her and she does not actually say a word. She just screams her head off down the telephone – and all I hear is my family in the background, a massive entourage, screaming with her! I tell her I will call her later.

I speak to all the media guys. They are really happy for me and then it is time for the presentation. But I am so exhausted. Bryan is there as usual with my kit. He has been so good, he looks after me. He has been great helping me deal with things. I can rely on him. He tells me how brilliantly I have done. The pain took a lot out of me. I am really dizzy and light-headed. I sit down, I am tired. He gets me some water while other people are all buzzing around.

We are called to the presentation, much quicker than for the 800 metres, and Maria Cioncan is really happy with the fact she has a bronze medal (Tatyana Tomashova is second). I have two flags around me this time. All the British people are flying their flags again from the top of the stand that I look at as we go out for the presentation. It is brilliant.

I am in a total daze. I feel weird, like I have been taken over by another body. I cannot take in what I have done. I am shaking my head. In the 800 metres the British crowd were chanting my name. I did not cry then when it happened. But this time is different. As the national anthem is played, all the British fans are joining in but I cannot get the words out. I am choked up, but I am not going to breakdown. Cioncan does, she is overwhelmed, she is crying throughout the whole thing. I well up quite a lot. I have the other flag around my shoulders; it is such a special moment.

I leave the stadium to go to the press conference. I am in there being asked questions but I am so tired. I have no energy, everything has left me.

Then everyone shouts: 'Did you see that?'

On the television by the side in the room, our 4 x 100 metres guys have won gold. Two journalists jump up and run out. Charming!

Earlier on it seemed like they could do it, the talent we have for sprinting in Britain is fantastic. It is an amazing night.

I am asked how I feel. I cannot answer; I do not know what to say.

I go to my drugs test and combine it with a blood test. You have to provide 120 millilitres. I end up with only 95. I have to stay to repeat the sample and

I am here for another hour or so. I drink what seems like a ton of water and soft drinks, waiting with everyone else and there are loads are athletes here. I do what it is needed –it has become a joke!

I leave. Margo and Zara are here. I hug them both.It is brilliant,they are so excited.

I give the flowers from the presentation to Margo and then I am needed for some media things.

Outside of the stadium, there are all these television stations lined up to talk to me. SKY have my mum on the phone line and I speak to her again.Then I go across to the BBC studio. Matthew Pinsent is there too. I talk about the whole night and the significance of what I have done, and what he did in winning his fourth rowing gold medal the week before. It is a really great interview.

Eventually I get back to the village – and I want to go out to celebrate. I have finished. It is my final night.

I hope to meet up with everyone but Ali has already gone out straight from the stadium. By the time I get back it is so late. Matt Elias and Catherine Murphy (fellow British athletes) come across to my apartment. It is 2.00 a.m. We try to leave the camp.There are no taxis. I phone Ali; we are still waiting.

Now it is 3.00 a.m. and Tamsyn Lewis meets up with us. We give up. Catherine and I go back. We are in the dining hall. It is 3.45 a.m. and I haven't even eaten. I sit there to 4.30 a.m. – what a great way to celebrate! I return to my block. I go out onto the balcony. It is 5.00 a.m. I call my mum. She is making a bit of sense this time but I haven't woken her. Back home they are all still up too, celebrating on my behalf. Amazing!

My Olympics is over. I do not know it at the time but tomorrow I will be given the honour of carrying the British flag at the closing ceremony. I could not have asked for a better ten days – such perfection.

71

The Elite Club

It did of course not dawn on me before the Olympic Games that I would become a member of a rare club in athletics. Only two women and a handful of men have won the 800 metres and 1,500 metres at the Olympic Games and to think I now rank alongside them is another incredible twist to my story.

But even more amazing is that I have succeeded in the footsteps of Ann Packer, who I think of as a true legend in British athletics. It was 40 years ago when she won the 800 metres in Tokyo and no other British woman since then has won a middle distance title at the Olympics Games until me. She, of course, did not have the opportunity to go for the middle distance double because it was not possible, as the 1,500 metres for women was not introduced until eight years later in Munich.

From a British viewpoint, to think that not even Seb Coe (he of the shoelaces), Steve Ovett, Steve Cram, Peter Elliott, the greats of British running, achieved what I did is amazing. The middle distance double has been achieved by one British man. His name was Albert Hill and his story is extraordinary. It was why, after my win on the Saturday night when I triumphed in the 1,500 metres in Athens, so much historical resonance was put on what I did. It has been 84 years since he won the 800 metres and 1,500 metres in Antwerp and, as we shall find out, it was an incredible story.

From an international point of view, Tatyana Kazankina and Svetlana Masterkova are Russian distance running legends. If someone had told me in 1996 in Atlanta, when I finished fourth in the 800 metres behind Masterkova and eleventh in the 1,500 metres, that in eight years' time I would be achieving what she did, I would not have believed them. But, in a tribute to what I achieved, here are all of their stories. I wonder if it will be another 84 years before a Briton does it again. I hope not. But in a way it puts into context what I achieved. A rare feat.

ANN PACKER
Born: 8 March 1942, Berkshire, England
Olympic record: 1964: gold:
800 metres, silver: 400 metres.

Ann Packer went to the Olympic Games in Tokyo with the 400 metres as her main event, but she left having caused one of the surprises of the Games by winning the 800 metres – a woman who triumphed over the two laps despite having no international experience of the distance. This was true to such an extent that when she ran in the first round heat, it was only the sixth time she had run the event. But her speed in the 400 metres, where she had set a European record of 52.0 but came second, came into use in the 800 metres as, amazingly, she charged home in 2:01.1, an Olympic and European record.

So was born one of the greats of British athletics and the Olympics. It was the first time that a British woman had won a track event at the Games and it so easily might not have happened.

Packer was thinking of not even running in the final of the 800 metres and going shopping instead. She changed her mind after Robbie Brightwell, her fiancé, came only fourth in the 400 metres. She decided to make up for what happened to him and it worked.

'I was thinking about him,' she said, 'and not about myself, so I wasn't nervous. It was so easy. I could not believe I won.'

What a story! It was some race. Maryvonne Dupureur of France had broken the Olympic record in the semi-final when she ran 2:04.1 and she led in the final, only for Packer to go past her in the home straight.

Years later, Packer recalled her triumph. 'Before Tokyo, I had run the 800 metres twice,' she said. 'I had moved up from sprints and jumping to the 400 metres. But I ran a couple of 800s for stamina preparation. I achieved the qualifying time and put down for the 800 as a third British girl.'

She became the first lady of the track, but it was her final race. She married Brightwell and both were awarded MBEs in 1969 and, until this year, no British woman had won a middle distance event at the Olympics.

ALBERT HILL
Born: 24 March 1889, London, England
Died: 8 January 1969, Canada
Olympic record: 1920: gold,
800 metres, 1,500 metres;
1924: silver, 3,000 metres

Even to this day Albert Hill remains one of the great characters of British Olympics, and with a worldwide impact too. No man has ever won the 800 metres or the 1,500 metres at the age he was.

Hill triumphed at the Olympic Games in Antwerp in 1920 when he was 31 and he did it using some of the most unconventional methods you could imagine.

He ran for Gainsford AC and Polytechnic Harriers and served in the First World War. Even though in 1920 he was back in Europe for happier reasons, he was still not convinced about one thing: he had suffered illness and stomach upsets during his time in France and Belgium during the War because of the water he drank, so he prepared for the Games ... by drinking Belgian lager.

It worked. He was a runner made of steel. He had five races in five days, no rehydration packs like us, and he won both gold medals in an amazing way.

Hill won his first gold in the 800 metres just half an hour after the semi-finals. He triumphed in 1:53.4. Then, in the 1,500 metres, he was helped by his British team mate Philip Baker, who ran alongside him and helped to hold off the field. Hill won in 4:01.8. Baker was second in 4:02.3.

Baker famously went on to enjoy a political career, becoming Lord Noel-Baker and in 1959 he was awarded the Nobel Peace Prize for promoting international disarmament.

Amazingly, not until Peter Snell of New Zealand won the middle distance double in Tokyo in 1964, the same place where Ann Packer triumphed, did anyone else achieve it again.

Just hearing about Hill's triumphs show how the sport has changed. In 1920 the Olympics was hardly the spectacular event it is now and, even though he was 31, his age had almost cost him his place at the Games. In 1920 he had run only the 880 yards and the selectors believed he was too old for the Olympics. In particular, Sir Harry Barclays, Secretary of the AAA, did not want him in the team, and the runner thought he had lost his trip across the Channel.

But Hill protested that he was good enough, a claim he proved with two stupendous performances in the finals.

He had first caught their eye ten years earlier when he won the AAA four miles title, but his athletics career was halted when he served in France as a signalman with the Royal Flying Corps.

After the war he won the AAA 880 yards and mile titles in 1919, equalling the British record for the latter of 4:16.8.

He had two coaches: the famous long distance runner Walter George and the legendary Sam Mussabini, the guru who advised Harold Abrahams to win his 100 metre Chariots Of Fire triumph in the 1924 Olympics. Hill himself became a successful coach after he had retired, guiding Britain's Sydney Wooderson to the 800 metres world record in 1938. He moved to Canada prior to the start of World War Two and died in January 1969, one of the true legends.

TATYANA KAZANKINA
Born: 17 December 1951, Petrovsk, Russia
Olympic record: 1976: gold, 800 metres,
1,500 metres; 1980: gold: 1,500 metres

Women had run the 1,500 metres at the Olympic Games only once before, at the 1972 Games in Munich, but this Russian took the race to a new level in Montreal. She broke the world record for the 800 metres by more than a second and became the first woman to achieve the middle distance double.

The 800 metres came first in Montreal but the 1,500 metres was very much her specialist event. On 26 July she stormed away to win a world record in the shorter distance to allow herself the opportunity to go for the double.

Kazankina had been entered into the 800 metres only at the last moment, but she won in 1:54.94 from Bulgaria's Shtereva Nikolina, who was second in 1:55.42.

In the last 50 metres of a tremendous race, where a fast pace had been set from the start, she moved from fifth place to first to win.

Four days later it was the final of the 1,500 metres, and it was run just the way Kazankina liked it. A slow start, a tactical confrontation as these races so often are, but she was the overall favourite. Just over a month earlier she had broken the world record for the 1,500 metres when she ran 3:56.0 with a stunning run where she lowered the record time by 5.4 seconds. It had been a record that was set by Lyudmila Bragina of the Soviet Union in Munich as she won the Olympic title four years earlier.

Bragina was back to defend her title and she was not going to give it up easily. She led until just past the bell, when she was overtaken by Gunhild Hoffmeister and Ulrike Klapezynski of East Germany, but Kazankina was in control. She was cool, steering clear of the elbowing and bustling that was taking place and she moved through to win in 4:05.48. She retained the 1,500 metres title four years later in Munich, but it would be twenty years until the double feat would be repeated.

SVETLANA MASTERKOVA
BORN: 17 January 1968, Achinsk
Sibirien, Russia
Olympic record: 1996: gold: 800 metres,
1,500 metres

Masterkova's fellow Russian Kazankina had set the standard and, though many tried in the intervening years at the Olympics, no one could match it. But then, in Atlanta in 1996, it happened again with the spectacular Masterkova showing thrilling quality to win the double. This achievement saw her honoured in 2004 by the International Association Of Athletics Federations for her contribution to sport.

She was a runner packed with power. Her fair hair would flow in the wind and in Atlanta she was just too good for anyone else.

What made her stand out was that she achieved her glory during the latter part of a career. In 1991 she ran the fastest time in the world that year: 1:57.23. In 1995 she left the sport to give birth to her daughter. Within sixteen months she was in the record books

as a double Olympic champion. It was some comeback. When she raced for the first time in an event in France two months before the 1996 Olympics, it was her first competition for almost three years.

She had a constant battle with weight, with pregnancy having an effect. Many women distance runners say that giving birth has a major effect on the body, improving your speed and your endurance, and Masterkova proved that by winning in such style in Atlanta.

She had been mainly an 800 metre runner but the 1,500 metres was proof of her ability to step up a distance, despite being older and now a mother. She decided as she headed towards the Olympics that she would never eat after 2 p.m. – and her reward for such a diet was two gold medals. She won the 800 metres in 1:57.73, leading from the start in an event which included the brilliant Ana Quirot of Cuba, who was second in 1:58.11 with Maria Mutola of Mozambique third in 1:58.71.

Masterkova had an amazing ability to surge when it mattered and she did that effectively in the home straight to triumph. One week later, one gold became two for a runner who had hardly competed in the 1,500 metres. She won the race with 200 metres to go, crossing the line in 4:00.83 ahead of Gabriela Szabo, of Romania, who was second in 4:01.54 with Austria's Theresia Kiesl third in 4:03.02.

Tributes

LORD SEBASTIAN COE, Olympic Champion, 1,500 metres, 1980 & 1984

'Well, she did it. And she did it with style. Kelly did not put a foot wrong throughout the Athens Olympics, from the heats of the 800 metres to the final of the 1,500 metres. She ran foot-sure in the heats, qualifying in style and sending out all the right messages to her competitors. And she did it with an economy of effort. This allowed her to peak again in the final and run with fresh legs.

I think her great achievement – and this is where the double has eluded a lot of athletes including myself, Steve Ovett and Steve Cram – is on the mental side. It would have been easy for her to have spent the day off between the semi-final and the final looking back at what she had done, rather than looking ahead to the battle to be fought. She won the battle with a knockout. At no stage had she allowed doubt to play a part.

I was in the stadium to watch her 1,500 metres and it was a bit like watching a film with the script in your hand. As the race unfolded I found myself muttering things like 'move out' and 'don't get trapped', but before I could get the words out she had done it. Her on-board computer was programmed absolutely perfectly.

She has entered an elite level; she is going to be known and recognised by everyone everywhere she goes in this country. She will now be ranked alongside the greatest Olympians such as Michael Johnson, Haile Gebrselassie and Hicham El Gerrouj.

But, I think my abiding memory will be from the tunnel after the 800 metres when there was a half an hour delay before the medal ceremony due to an appeal for second and third place. Kelly and I waited together. She looked shocked and dumbstruck. She couldn't comprehend what she had achieved and was shaking. Kelly reminded me of one of my own kids, shivering on the beach after being in the sea too long. The athlete in me took over as I urged her to take her spikes off and warm down. She was beyond communicating so I undid her shoelaces. Yolanda Ceplak, who came third, took her arm and pulled her off to the warm-up area. I was very lucky and hugely honoured to share these unique moments with her.'

SALLY GUNNELL, Olympic Champion, 400 metres hurdles, 1992

'When Kelly Holmes walked out into the stadium for the final of the women's 800 metres the tension was almost unbearable. I hoped that underneath that cool exterior she was calm and ready for the big challenge ahead. The gun went and I found myself screaming at her like every other British supporter. With 200 metres to go I watched her unleash an amazing sprint, it was a wonderful sight to see her fighting for first place down the finishing straight and crossing the line for the gold medal position. There were tears in my eyes – all those years of injuries and hard work had been worth it for her to have achieved her big ambition. It was fantastic to watch her on her lap of honour – British flags everywhere – so much noise! It brought back so many great memories of my own Olympic success. As she approached me I will never forget such tears of happiness. I gave her a big hug and just thought I cannot let everyone back home see us crying our eyes out. If anybody deserves that gold it's Kelly. The hard work, the perseverance – and also for being a nice person. She will still be the same old Kel at the end of the day. I had to go through all those emotions again when she went and won the 1,500 metres as well!!!

STEVE CRAM MBE, Olympic silver medalist, 1,500 metres, 1984

'As a commentator you always strive to be as impartial as possible but every now and then that all goes out of the window. In the 800 metres final as Kelly hit the front in the home straight I couldn't help but get completely carried away with the emotion and excitement of what was happening. A big part of me still thinks like an athlete and I was trying to scream Kelly to the finish line. She made it and as she was trying desperately to confirm what she didn't dare think, there was I like an idiot trying to talk to her from the commentary box.

It was a great privilege to have been commentating on what will undoubtedly rank as one of the most memorable Olympic achievements ever.'

RICHARD LEWIS BIOG:
Richard Lewis is the Executive Editor of *Athletics Weekly* and he has been reporting on athetics for more than 20 years. He is a former athletics correspondent of the *Daily Express* and now covers the sport for the *Sunday Times*. Athens was his fourth Olympic Games and he has followed Kelly Holmes' career from the start.

PICTURE CREDITS:
pp. 1, 2, 20, 23, 29, 30, 40-1, 46, 71 (middle), 77
Courtesy of Action Images

pp. 7, 9, 11, 73, 76, 78, 79 (left)
Courtesy of Corbis

p. 75 Courtesy of Empics

Endpapers and pp. 52, 74, 79 (right)
Courtesy of Getty Images

pp. 12-13, 38-9, 44, 54, 58, 62, 68-9, 71 (top and bottom), 80
Courtesy of Mark Shearman, Athletics Images

pp. 4, 26 Courtesy of PA Photos